Fiesta!
joyous pieces for organ

kevin mayhew

We hope you enjoy the music in this book.
Further copies of this and our many other books are available
from your local Kevin Mayhew stockist.

In case of difficulty, or to request a catalogue,
please contact the publisher direct by writing to:

The Sales Department
KEVIN MAYHEW LTD
Buxhall
Stowmarket
Suffolk IP14 3BW

Phone 01449 737978
Fax 01449 737834
E-mail info@kevinmayhewltd.com

First published in Great Britain in 2003 by Kevin Mayhew Ltd.

© Copyright 2003 Kevin Mayhew Ltd.

ISBN 1 84417 163 9
ISMN M 57024 257 3
Catalogue No: 1400352

0 1 2 3 4 5 6 7 8 9

The music in this book is protected by copyright and may not be reproduced
in any way for sale or private use without the consent of the copyright owner.

Cover design: Angela Selfe
Music setter: Geoffrey Moore

Printed and bound in Great Britain

Contents

		Page
A joyful 'going out'	Colin Mawby	44
Carillon on 'Llanfair'	Andrew Wright	59
Commuter caprice	Richard Lloyd	38
Exultate Deo	Rosalie Bonighton	15
Fanfare with trio	Simon Lesley	34
Finale	Michael Higgins	22
Flourish for the tuba	June Nixon	48
Marche française	Andrew Fletcher	18
Marche grotesque	John Jordan	31
Onwards and upwards	Judith Bailey	5
Postlude	Andrew Moore	46
Sculpture	Timothy Blinko	8
Season's joy	Betty Roe	50
Spirito	Stanley Vann	53
Toccatina	Robert Jones	26
Triumphal march	Norman Warren	56

About the Composers

Judith Bailey (*b*.1941) has taught at various colleges and has been a tutor for the Open University and Workers' Educational Association. She was conductor of the Southampton Concert Orchestra and Petersfield Orchestra for thirty years and since 1993 has worked entirely as a composer and conductor.

Timothy Blinko (*b*.1965) was Bliss scholar at the Royal College of Music, becoming Head of Composition at the Royal College's junior department in 1994, and the first Associate Head of Music at the University of Hertfordshire in 2001. In 2003 Timothy also became Director of Music at Ealing Abbey.

Rosalie Bonighton (*b*.1946) is a composer, part-time teacher, and Organist and Music Director at St John the Evangelist Church, Ballarat, Australia. She writes for both professional and amateur performers, and has a special interest in music for liturgical needs.

Andrew Fletcher (*b*.1950) is a Midlands-based church musician, choral director, teacher, composer, arranger and concert organist who regularly gives recitals, masterclasses and choral workshops both in England and the USA.

Michael Higgins (*b*.1981) is currently studying music at the Birmingham Conservatoire. He regularly accompanies soloists and choral societies, including the National Children's Choir of Great Britain.

Robert Jones lives in Monmouth. Having taught for over thirty years he is now retired, but, in addition to composing, continues to be active as an organist, accompanist and examiner.

John Jordan (*b*.1941) was for many years Master of the Music at Chelmsford Cathedral. He now combines being Music Director of St Margaret's Priory Church, King's Lynn, and Director of Music at the national shrine of Our Lady of Walsingham.

Simon Lesley (*b*.1974) is an award-winning composer, organist and trombonist. He lectures in composition at Birmingham. His arrangements and compositions are widely published.

Richard Lloyd (*b*.1933) was Assistant Organist of Salisbury Cathedral and successively Organist of Hereford and Durham Cathedrals. He now divides his time between examining and composing.

Colin Mawby (*b*.1936) has achieved an international reputation as a composer. His vocal writing is widely acknowledged to be 'masterly' and his music 'inspirational'. He was for many years Master of Music at Westminster Cathedral.

Andrew Moore studied at the Royal Academy of Music and at Cambridge University. He is currently parish priest of St Francis, Ascot.

June Nixon is one of Australia's best-known organists, choir trainers and composers. She is Organist and Director of Music at St Paul's Cathedral, Melbourne, and teaches at the Music Faculty of Melbourne University.

Betty Roe (*b*.1930) Studied music at the Royal Academy of Music and composition with Lennox Berkeley. Best known for her music in the community, her works include many musicals for all ages, and four operas.

Stanley Vann (*b*.1910) was Assistant Organist at Leicester Cathedral and Chorus Master of Leicester Philharmonic for Sir Henry Wood and Sir Malcolm Sargent; later successively Organist at Chelmsford and Peterborough Cathedrals. Composer of eight Masses, fourteen Evening Services, many motets, anthems and organ pieces.

Norman Warren (*b*.1934) is a retired Archdeacon of Rochester. He is well known as a composer of hymns, and was a member of the music committee for *Hymns for Today's Church* and *Sing Glory*.

Andrew Wright (*b*.1955) studied music at Worcester College, Oxford, under Robert Sherlaw Johnson and was a former Assistant Master of Music at Westminster Cathedral. He has been Master of Music and Diocesan Director of Music for the Diocese of Brentwood since 1982 and is very active as a conductor, teacher, performer and composer. Compositions include motets, carols, liturgical music and organ music.

For Isabel

ONWARDS AND UPWARDS

Judith Bailey

Sw. 8' 4'
Gt. 8' 4'
Ped.16'

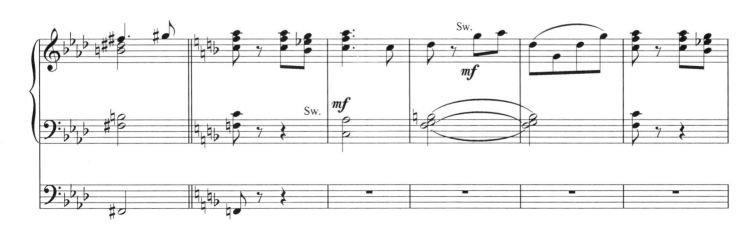

© Copyright 2003 Kevin Mayhew Ltd.
It is illegal to photocopy music.

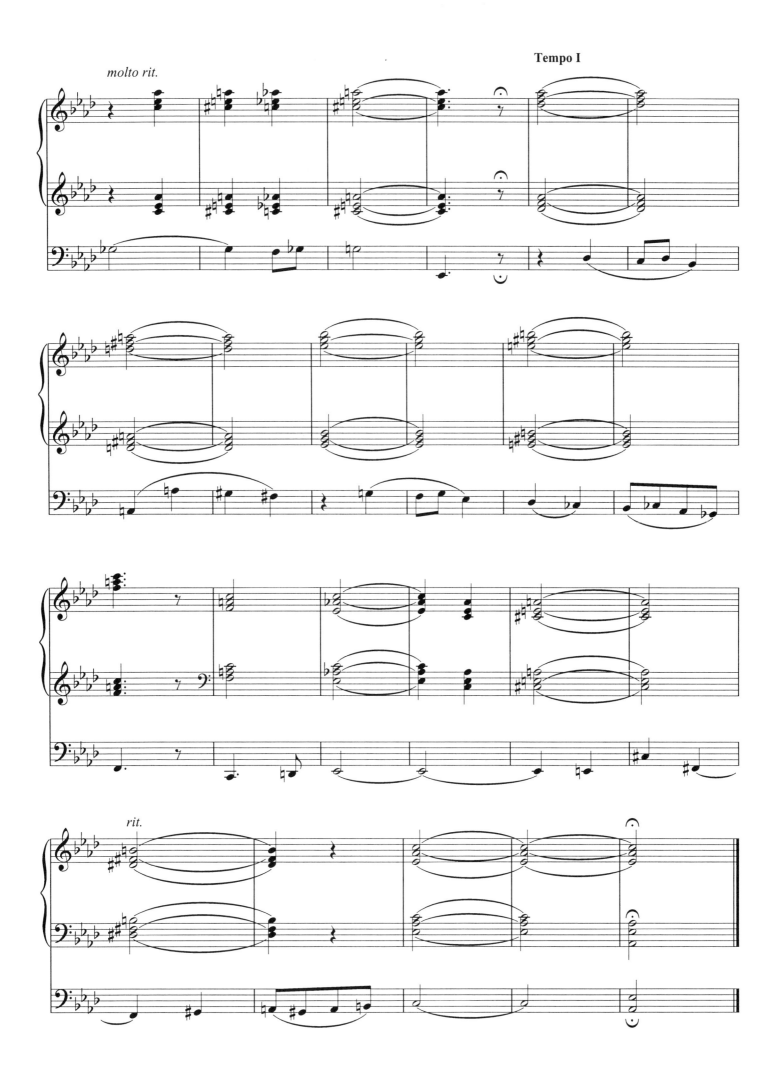

For Kevin Bowyer

SCULPTURE

Timothy Blinko

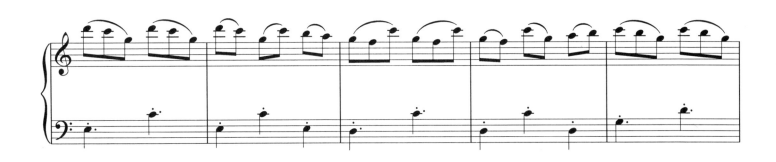

© Copyright 2003 Kevin Mayhew Ltd.
It is illegal to photocopy music.

EXULTATE DEO

Rosalie Bonighton

Interlude

MARCHE FRANÇAISE

Andrew Fletcher

© Copyright 2003 Kevin Mayhew Ltd.
It is illegal to photocopy music.

FINALE

Michael Higgins

It is illegal to photocopy music.

© Copyright 2003 Kevin Mayhew Ltd.
It is illegal to photocopy music.

TOCCATINA

Robert Jones

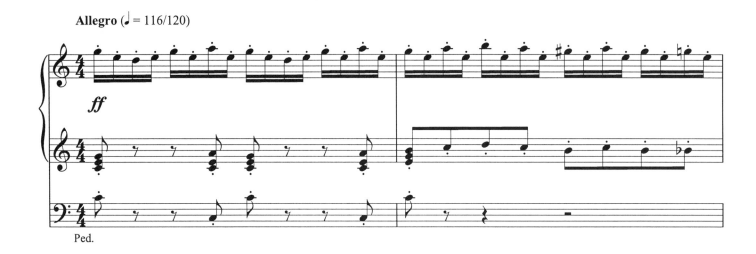

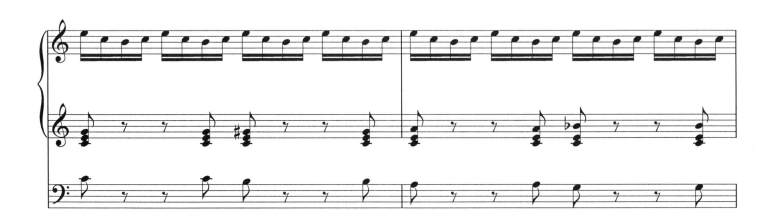

© Copyright 2003 Kevin Mayhew Ltd.
It is illegal to photocopy music.

MARCHE GROTESQUE

John Jordan

Pedal only for the repeat

Man.

© Copyright 2003 Kevin Mayhew Ltd.
It is illegal to photocopy music.

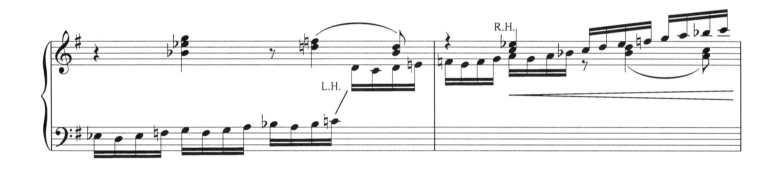

FANFARE WITH TRIO

Simon Lesley

© Copyright 2003 Kevin Mayhew Ltd.
It is illegal to photocopy music.

COMMUTER CAPRICE

Richard Lloyd

Con spirito e sperato

poco rit.

A JOYFUL 'GOING OUT'

Colin Mawby

POSTLUDE

Andrew Moore

FLOURISH FOR THE TUBA

June Nixon

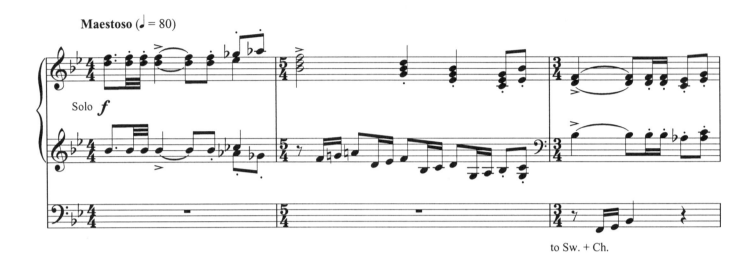

© Copyright 2003 Kevin Mayhew Ltd.
It is illegal to photocopy music.

For Mary and Gordon Hicks

SEASON'S JOY
Betty Roe

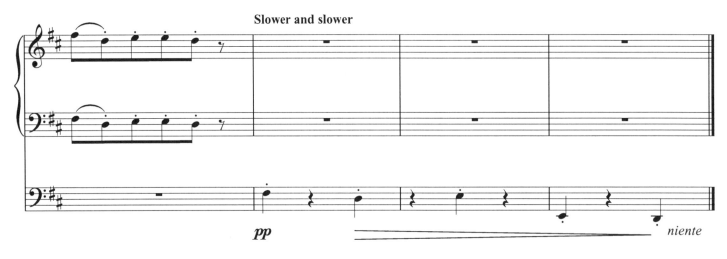

SPIRITO

Stanley Vann

TRIUMPHAL MARCH

Norman Warren

Prepare:
Sw. to Mixture
Gt. to 15th
Sw. to Gt.
Gt. to Ped.
Sw. to Ped.

© Copyright 2003 Kevin Mayhew Ltd.
It is illegal to photocopy music.

For the Feast of the Ascension

CARILLON ON 'LLANFAIR'

Andrew Wright

© Copyright 2003 Kevin Mayhew Ltd.
It is illegal to photocopy music.